Arthur Joseph Munby

Vestigia Vetrorsum

Poems

Arthur Joseph Munby

Vestigia Vetrorsum
Poems

ISBN/EAN: 9783337005818

Printed in Europe, USA, Canada, Australia, Japan

Cover: Foto ©Thomas Meinert / pixelio.de

More available books at **www.hansebooks.com**

VESTIGIA RETRORSUM

Poems

BY

ARTHUR J. MUNBY

LONDON
JOHN MACQUEEN
HASTINGS HOUSE, NORFOLK STREET, STRAND
1899

CONTENTS.

PAGE

LOVE LYRICS AND POEMS.

SONNETS.

NOTE.

A few of the sonnets in this volume are reprinted, with permission, from "The Academy." All the other pieces are now published for the first time. The sonnet on Beatrice is of special interest. At the invitation of the Italian Committee in charge of the recent Beatrice Exposition at Florence, meant to commemorate the first meeting of Dante and Beatrice, which happened in May, and the death of Beatrice, on June 9, 1290, many sonnets and other poems in honour of the occasion were written by Englishmen, Americans, and others, as well as by Italians ; and Miss R. H. Busk, whose intimate acquaintance with Italian life and Italian folk-lore made her a valuable ally, was good enough to represent the Committee in England, and to forward for their acceptance the poems written in England. The Beatrice sonnet in this volume is one of these. Along with numerous others, it was "diplomated" by the Italian Committee : a fact which, at any rate, shows that Mr. Munby's view of the storicità of Beatrice was not unacceptable.

"Vestigia Retrorsum" is a remarkable contrast to "Vulgar Verses," a book, written mainly in dialect, dealing with working folk only, and pro- jected almost entirely on their level of experience and attainment. Such a book, also,—but sketched from a higher point of view—is "Dorothy," a poem which has had wide acceptance in America, and has even achieved a certain measure of success in its own country. The present volume has nothing to do with hard hands, or female labour, or any such thing. It deals with gentler and loftier themes, dwelling on them in such moods as may be expected from one who is exercised by the questions of his own time, and saddened by the fast- fading, fast-narrowing beauties of the land he lives in.

The Editor is sorry that the elegiacs in this volume do not uniformly appear in self-contained lines. English elegiacs have as much right to the dignity of a broad page as a Greek or a Latin hexameter. It would not be well, however, to have volumes of different sizes in the same series.

W. EARL HODGSON.

London, May, 1891.

DESCRIPTIVE AND IMAGINATIVE.

THE VALES OF MEDWAY.

Spring ! She is with us again, in the air, in the stream,
in the wildwood ;
Giving the world once more freshness and odour and
joy :
Giving it more than these—the sense of a great
resurrection,
Life springing up out of death, hope overcoming
despair.
All mankind who dwell in the live and natural country,
Far from the toys and the trade, far from the arts of
a town,

All mankind who dwell in the presence of innocent
Nature,

Now are afield and alert, finding their forces anew :

Also the beasts and the birds, our quiet and happy
companions,

Fill'd with a new-found life, welcome existence
again.

Nature herself is alive; the infinite earthborn creatures

All come at once to the birth, struggle at once to be
born.

Oh, 'tis a thing to be seen, to be heard, to be felt,
to be ponder'd,

Such an uprising as this, old as the hills though it be.

Here on the Medway flood, where a hundred bright
little islands

Shine on the broad full tide, stars of its widespread-
  ing blue,
Here are the ships coming in, with sails fullset **to**
  the breezes,
Types of the hope that appears, fraught with adven-
  ture, to us:
And on the hundred isles, on the beautiful breast of
  the waters,
Sunlight gleams and glides, changed with the change-
  able clouds.
Here on the Medway hills, where the land slopes
  suddenly seaward,
Green grows the flush of the corn, moist with the
  lustre of dew.
Yes, and the old brown woods, though they seem
  still dead from a distance,
They too are filling with life, quick with the pulses
  of Spring:

Witness the steel-like sheen that glosses the bark of
the saplings,

Witness the tassell'd blooms hung from the willows
below.

What should I speak of the banks and the wild and
wandering hedgerows,

What of the lanes between, winding from village to
farm?

Beautiful they with buds, the red-nippled buds of the
hawthorn,

Harbouring too in the grass nests of the earliest
flowers.

Also by hamlet and fold, by many a trim cottage-
dwelling,

Each with its ivied porch, each with its old hooded well,

Daffodils nod at the gate, and wealth is abroad in the
garden —

Silver of snowdrop tufts, crocuses given for gold.

Now come away to the fields, where the men of the
country are working ;

Men—aye, and women too—working all day with a
will :

Here in the vale hard by, stout women are barking
the hop-poles ;

There are the men at plough, cheerily guiding the
teams ;

Yonder, where lasses and lads in summer time wend
to the milking,

Now they are standing a-row, each with her shovel
and sieve,

Opening the straw-cover'd hoard, where fodder is
kept through the winter,

Sifting the bad from the good, food for the cattle and
swine.

Hark ! from yon high grey Downs the tremulous
musical sheep-bells

Call us to come and behold all that our shepherds
can show;

Who with their low-wheel'd huts abide in the field
for the lambing,

Watching night and day over the weak of the fold.

Ah! from those high grey Downs, what a height,
what a scope, of enjoyment!

Songs of the mating birds heard in the hollows afar—

Songs of the lark in air, or the clamorous chirp of the
starlings,

Seated aloft in crowds, talking together at eve.

You who would know what it is to rejoice in the
beauty of England,

Come to these high grey Downs; come in an even-
ing of Spring —

Come in the Autumn noons, or come in a sweet
Summer morning —

Stand upon Darland Heights, gaze on the glories
  around !

Look to the east, far down, where the broad white
  Roman highway

Scores the green flank of the hills, stately and sound
  as of old :

Look to the east, far down, where Medway sweeps
  to the ocean,

Meeting the broader Thames, surging away to the
  Nore.

There, by the tall sea banks, by the low rich pastures
  of Essex,

There go the ships, far off, bearing the wealth of the
  world ;

Bearing it on with the tide, to the port and harbour
  of London,

Bearing it thence in turn out to the ocean again.

Near, o'er the Medway stream, look down on an
  humbler traffic —

Fishermen's craft alone, barges and boats of the
 shore:

Yes, and yon giant hulks, where soldiers live as in
 barracks,

Learning their terrible trade, disciplined daily to war.

Ah, look away from them, look away from the forts
 in the channel

(Needed and wanting once, soon to be needed again),

Look to the smiling shores, to the villages set in the
 woodland,

Orchards and red-roof'd farms, churches and castles
 and all.

Then to the west turn round, and see right on to the
 landward,

Fold upon fold, the hills rising like waves of the sea:

But at your feet, low down, lies the silent valley of
 Darland,

Winding in many a curve up to the highlands afar;

Steep are its purple sides, where folded flocks are
    a-slumber,

And on the further slope, warm in the depth of the
    vale,

Cluster'd hop-poles stand, like the tents of an army
    encamping,

Soon to be sever'd and ranged, soon to be leafy and
    green.

Over against us here, on the opposite height, on the
    summit,

Hempstead stands alone, grey with its gables and
    barns ;

And from Hempstead farm, right on to the western
    horizon,

Fold upon fold, our hills rise like the waves of the sea ;

Crested with high dim lawns, and tufted with copses
    and timber,

Till on the lucid sky loftier ridges appear.

Yes, that is Bluebell Hill, that far in the golden
distance

Looks over Maidstone town on to the Garden of
Kent;

Looks on those fallen fanes, that wonderful House
of the Druids,

Oldest of all things old now on the face of the land.

See, into this fair scene, these hills and valleys and
waters,

Comes the majestic sun, sobering down to his rest :

He, who was shining above, unapproachable sovereign
of all things,

Now, at the eventide, friendly, familiar and near,

Glows among purple clouds, his solemn and mourn-
ful attendants,

Dies as a King should die, gracious and calm to the
end.

Then, what a triumph of life, what a gorgeous
' apotheosis

Mounts from the place of his death up to the zenith
on high !

Then, what a blaze of light, of various infinite colour,

Out of his open tomb springs like a fountain of hope !

First, through those purple clouds, and under and in
and around them,

Bars of ruby red, vivid, intense as a flame ;

Paler crimson above, and mellowing softening saffron

Melt through a liquid green into the ultimate blue :

Up to the final blue, where clear cold stars are
awaiting,

Till with the luminous dark they shall have leave to
appear.

Come, come away—let us go ; let us saunter silently
homeward—

Under these clear cold stars, under this luminous sky ;

Thinking, with hearts that are full of enchanting
and exquisite beauty,

"Ah, what a land is this—ah, what an Eden is here!"

Yes—what an Eden is here, if men were able to
know it,

Able to see with their eyes, willing and able to feel!

But they are not: not a man, nor a child, nor even a
woman .

Cares that the land of their birth still should be pure
as of old.

What? If they loved greensward, sweet air, and
life-giving waters,

Would they stand mute, as they do, seeing all these
disappear?

Seeing their mountain-lakes fast stolen and spoilt by
the stranger,

Seeing the streams of the vale blacken'd and poison'd
    and foul;

Seeing the air they breathe, the needful breath of
    their nostrils,

Changed into filthiest gloom, acrid with sulphur and
    soot;

Seeing their hideous towns, their mean and comfort-
    less dwellings,

Sprawl o'er the innocent fields, ugly and aimless and
    bare:

Yes! for Beauty is dead, and the excellent craft of
    the builder

Fail'd, when the builder himself ceased to be honest
    and true.

What shall be done then for these—for a people
    besotted as this is,

Making such haste to be rich, caring for nothing but
  greed ?
Nay, if they will not turn, and ask of their fathers
  before them
How to discern the Good, whether in Nature or
  Art;
How to transmit it, increased by the labour of each
  generation,
Weeded of evil, indeed, but with a delicate hand ;
Never destroying a good, except for the sake of a
  better,
Hating the bad alone, keeping their vengeance for
  that :
Nay, if they will not turn, there is blackness of dark-
  ness before them ;
Lurid with lights that lead only to uttermost hell :
Indolence sapping their wealth, and cowardice offei'd
  for courage ;

Knowledge that is but a name—bastard of folly and
pride;

Peace trodden down by war; divine Humility
dying;

Reverence shamed with scorn; Love going out in
despair.

REALITIES.

Whenas the feebled sun is fading in the sky,
And trees forget their leavës brown which on the
    earth do lie;
When cattle stand in yard and sheep are in the fold,
I walk abroad, and with my heart this grave dis-
    course do hold.

Oh Heart, that livest long withouten love or joy,
Hast thou perceived what lovesome things great
    Winter doth destroy?
The summer clouds so fair, and shining of the sun
On golden corn in harvest days, are wholly past and
    gone:

The little birdës all, which build their nests in spring,

No more unto their merry makes at morningtide do

    sing;

And every flower so sweet in greenwood where it

    grew,

Hath lost its savour long ago, and all its pleasant hue.

Then, Heart, consider well, and sadly say to me

If these so happy things must die, what shall be

    done for thee?

I would 'twere done for me (thus doth my Heart

    reply)—

That same which shall be done for them when Spring

    is in the sky!

But thou, beholding thus the creatures from afar,

Hast neither eyes to see nor wit to know them as

    they are.

For as a field doth lie beneath the plower's hand,

To drive therein his furrows smooth across the yield-
ing land;

Or as the sower's grain that 'twixt each furrow lies,

According as he sow'd the seed, shall certainly arise:

Right so, with soulless things, God maketh them to
know

Within themselves what thing to do, and in what
wise to grow;

But me, that am His child, and foster'd for His own,

He will not tell me what shall be—He leaveth me
alone!

I may not hear thee thus, thou villain Heart and base;

Some light of God is surely there within thy dwelling-place;

And if thou art to fade, and wither and decay,

So also do those happy things before they pass away.

Nay (saith my Heart, and sighs), if that were all, I
  ween

Thou should'st not hear me sighing sore for trouble
  and for tene :

But look now toward the west, and toward the east
  also,

And see how still this Earth doth lie a-waiting for
  the snow !

Her working year is done; her deeds are with her
  there;

Upon her breast her children all lie orderly and fair;

Her grain is garner'd in, her flowers live in seed,

Her fruits are stored in chambers sweet for cyder or
  for mead ;

Her kine shall calve again, her ewes grow great with
  young—

Her birdës shall sing blithe to her as ever they have
  sung ;

And every living thing once more shall have his fere,

And unto every living thing his make be lief and dear.

For why? Her life is led by reason and by rule;

She hath no need to learn her babes, nor put their
wits to school :

They know their parts aright, they are not fools and
blind,

But apt to lead their little lives according to their kind;

And if there be of hers some stubborn froward child,

She helpeth well the husbandman to make him nesh
and mild.

So thus it comes to pass, as wretched men may see,

That Earth and all her soulless ones are blest in their
degree:

They ask not where to go, nor think that aught can
cease,

They only walk in God His ways—and all His ways
are peace.

But thou (my Heart did say), which talkest thus
    with me,

I know thy mind doth work apace, and will not let
    thee be :

And for myself, to tell 'twere pity and 'twere pain

The tithe of what I have endured, and must endure
    again.

For me, no later Spring shall rouse the birdës small,

Nor fetch forth buds on that old tree which long ago
    did fall;

For me, no cunning hand shall sift the wheat and straw,

Nor ever from the musty lees a mellow mead shall draw.

I move, where'er I go, whatever things I see,

Among the wreck of hopes and joys which once
    were part of me;

And what is lost, is lost: who mourneth, then, but I,

Which know that Sorrow endeth not, and Passion
    will not die?

WORDSWORTH.

In Nature still
Glorying, I found a counterpoise in her
Which, when the spirit of evil reached its height,
Maintain'd for me a secret happiness.—
The Prelude, Book xii.

She, whom we loved and courted in our youth,

And courted not, yet loved unconsciously,

While the bad world was with us, and all truth,

Pity, and grace had almost ceased to be:

Nature, mild guardian of the wise and good,

Friend of the meek and lowly, and by whom

True manhood lives and pious maidenhood,

To her, to her, we will return at last,

Repentant of our follies and our crimes.

Ah, what an irrecoverable Past,

What dreary days and nights of grief and gloom,

    Since those far-off but unforgotten times

When she was mistress of the opening soul—

    She, Nature, and the God that guideth her!

Smooth and uncheck'd the sacred seasons roll,

    And after all this fret and fume and stir

Of middle life, its hurry and its care,

    Spring lays her blossoms on the old man's heart

As if it were a maid's.   But can he bear

    That fragrant burden?   Every year, a part

Of what in him was touch'd with vernal joy

    And warm'd by summer suns, is dying down,

Till autumn finds no leafage to destroy,

    And winter, only winter, is his own :

Winter, not glowing in the pure delight

    Of new-faln snow, the fancy and the pride

Of icicle and wreathen-drift, made bright

    With morning, or by solemn sunsets dyed

In splendour of their own ; but dusk and dim—

Dark with foul ways and many a shadow made

By storm-cloud, and with chill remembrance grim

Of powers misspent and sympathies decay'd.

Yet from decay may grow the better mind.

One man alone, in this at least supreme

O'er all the generations of his kind,

Beheld deliverance : not as in a dream,

But with the clear-eyed certainty of noon

Beheld and heard it.   Long with reverent ear

He heard the secrets of the sun and moon,

Stars, earth, and sea, the mountain and the mere,

And told of them to others; and to me,

Who, blest with sight of his serene old age,

Saw for myself, with what sweet majesty

Nature endow'd her poet and her sage.

Far be the strife of envious sects, and far

The grasping outrage of felonious trade,

And all things else that could defile or mar,

  From that green turf whereof his grave is made—

His grave, where lilies grow and daffodils,

  Fast by the murmur of the stream he loved

In Grasmere, guarded by his native hills.

  For he it was, who never once removed

(After the great catastrophe, the fall

  Of France, that shook his being to the core)

His faith from that which underlies us all;

  From Nature, whatsoever shape she bore,

Or aspect, grave and gloomy, glad and gay—

  From Nature, and the God that guideth her.

He never left the consecrated way

  That best became him as her minister:

So, not unmindful of the Cross of Christ

  And Him who hung thereon, his verse supplies

Airs of the elder Heaven, fresh breezes spiced

  With odours from that sinless Paradise

Where Man was rear'd, and might be dwelling still
   If Woman had obey'd. Ah, what avails
Obedience now, to uncreate our ill
   In woman or in man ?

               Yet *this* avails—
His teaching, and the eyes wherewith he saw,
   If we could have like insight ; it avails
To follow him, pure prophet of our law,
   Priest and exemplar of the creed we own.
If friends depart, if riches use their wings,
   If love decay'd should leave us all alone,
Are we alone ? Oh, no ! Far better things,
   Even on this earth, are with us if we choose.
Age cannot spoil, nor Sorrow's self destroy
   Our blessing, have we courage but to use
The sympathy, the comfort, and the joy
   That Nature, only Nature, can confer ;
Whose heart, whose voice, whose features, all employ
   In us, the good that God employs in her.

MILESTONES.

We rode, we rode, Bay Beauty and I,

When a sweet spring morn and an opal sky

    Spoke well for the things to come;

And Beauty fear'd nor fleck nor foam—

For the white road, set in its soft turf, seem'd

Like a Milky Way that glitter'd and gleam'd

    Right on to the heaven of home.

Bay Beauty, my steed, was swift and strong;

And she glanced and gazed, as we moved along,

    With a clear untroubled eye :

For Beauty, perhaps, was wiser than I—

But hers is an innocent creature's plan,

Which a man with a soul, a thinking man,

    Would be rash indeed to try.

The first mile out, we came to a dell,

Where children play'd round a village well,

    And women came forth to draw :

Bay Beauty was pleased with the folk she saw—

But she saw not the children's stunted lives,

Nor the mothers who never were wedded wives,

    Nor the drunkard's murderous paw.

The next mile out was a charming spot,

Made fair with the fair forget-me-not

    That grew by a river side :

Two lovers there Bay Beauty eyed—

But she knew not that even if love be true,

There are festering follies that sunder in two

    The bridegroom and the bride.

The next mile out, we pass'd through a town,

Where some were hooting and hunting down,

    And some were harried like hares :

Bay Beauty look'd on with her prancing airs—

Yet this is the way how men agree

With those who seek to be wise or free

    In a way that is not theirs.

The next mile out was a gruesome sight ;

For a sombre man, with a face like a blight,

    Had a message, he said, to tell :

Bay Beauty started, and it was well—

For as she sprang from him, the message I heard

Was nothing at all but a single word,

    And that single word was—Hell.

Oh, fast and far from that prophet of ill,

By heath and hollow, by holt and hill,

    Bay Beauty fled with me :

Her spirit was fresh, and her pace was free—

Though never a milestone came in view

But something to scorn, or something to rue

    Our eyes were sure to see.

There were those who suffer, and those who sting,

And the gay that weep, and the sad that sing,

    And the wicked who dwell at ease:

Bay Beauty and I look'd over the leas—

But she saw nothing, and I saw this :

That there was not the ghost of a Nemesis

    Following after these.

And we saw by the road, from mile to mile,

The rich man's house with its insolent smile

    Standing stable and sure:

And we saw men striving to kill or cure—

By making or mending of rules and laws

Amid hostile yells or fond applause—

    The perishing and the poor.

And we saw those wounds which the selfish rage

And the grasping greed of a vulgar age

    To our piteous Earth has given :

I think it shock'd Bay Beauty even—
Beholding the ruin of rural shades,
And the shameless plying of sordid trades
    At the very gates of heaven.

Alas! for the man who rides ahead
Till his brain grows dim and his heart grows dead
    With a hope too long deferr'd :
The hope of a voice that is never heard—
The calm pure voice and the flawless light
Of stately Justice, and conquering Right,
    And Love's almighty word!

But the last mile out I remember well;
For there Bay Beauty stumbled and fell,
    And struck me as I lay :
She struck me once and gallop'd away—
And I vow'd to God that I would not rise,
Till a spirit be in me to make me wise,
    At the Resurrection day.

D

Bay Beauty, my steed, has never come back;

She gallop'd away on her own white track

    To her own untroubled home:

She is freed from the rein and the crimson foam—

And I lie here in my lonely grave

Till I crawl out hence, like a startled slave,

    Into the Life to come.

THE WIDOWER.

Man that is born of woman dwells
Not wholly, as my story tells,
Among his business of the day;
But Fancy hurries him away,
And Hope looks forth, and Memory
Is busy with the things that die.

•

So, often when the working brain
Is stirr'd through pleasure into pain,
When Fame or Fortune, dearly bought
By stress of action or of thought,
Have left no leisure, while we strive,
For men to feel themselves alive;

E'en then (and how much more when they

Who make the strife are far away)

I too am led, but not by Hope,

High up the visionary slope

That leads to Heaven, and to her

Who once was Heaven's own minister.

I think she did not die too soon :

For on that night the harvest moon

Shone clear upon our gather'd sheaves;

And here and there the aspen leaves

That nestled near her window pane

Were touch'd already with the stain

Of autumn's beautiful decay.

Also, what time she pass'd away

We all were with her; on the bed

Her father and her mother shed

Their tears; her child was there, and I—

I too, could see my darling die.

Yes, friend, she did not die too soon :

She might have lived till every moon

That rose within our wedded years

Brought only trouble—only tears ;

She might have seen her child go wrong ;

Might have survived so much, so long,

That all which had been sweet and good—

The honey of our daily food—

Was emptied from its clammy comb,

And home itself no longer home.

Who, reasoning on the solid ground

Of things within him and around,

And judging by the sunder'd lives

Of fifty husbands, fifty wives,

Can say it would not have been so ?

And then, this is a world of woe :

Had we two loved and kept our truth

As dearly as we did in youth

Through fifty years of wedlock, say,

What then? Th' inevitable day

Were all the harder to be borne

When one of us is left forlorn

Of such a long beatitude.

Ah, so you tell me! And my mood

Persuades you that I do not grieve

Too much, it seems : you don't perceive,

Now she is dead, that I fulfil

My days with less of sober skill

To make a living, than before :

I do not cry behind the door

Like girls; nor blubber in the street;

Nor make wry faces when we meet :

And if I love my child, why yet

I never nurse that puny pet

As if its little face could be

Half what its mother's was, to me.

No! I'm not broken—scarcely sad :
And you, good friend, are very glad
I am so settled and so calm ;
You think I must have found the balm
That tempers to our mortal sense
These hard results of Providence.

Well—each one has his grieving fit,
And each his way of bearing it :
But, do you know, the death, the life,
Of her who was and is my wife
Are on me every day and hour
With even more of plastic power
Than when she was alive.   You stare :
My friend, it is not everywhere
Grown men will show their feelings ; **she**
Who is the better part of me
She knew them, and she knows them, all.
What do I care for grave or pall?

For those who faint and those who fail

The world within us is a veil,

Thank God, to hide the world without:

There is no shadow of a doubt

In me, when I am all alone,

No least mistrust, no lightest tone

Of sorrow, that can shake or stir

The heart which I have left with her.

REFLECTIVE.

JUSTICE.

Starry Justice sits on high
Clear above the clouded sky
    Judging men.
We shall see her, you and I;
We shall know her by-and-bye:
    Ah, but when?

When she severs good from ill;
Sifts the motive and the will
    From the deed;
Sets them with unerring skill
In her own calm light, until
    All can read.

REFLECTIVE.

When she looks with scornful eyes
On the wisdom of the wise,
    And her sword
Cleaving through each brave disguise
Bares and quells the enemies
    Of the Lord.

When she lays the tyrant low;
When her mission'd lightnings go
    Fierce and strong
Through the world, that all may know
Saint from sinner, friend from foe,
    Right from wrong.

When she lifts the trodden poor;
Opens wide her palace door
    As they come
To the peaceful and the pure;
Making these for ever sure
    In her home.

REFLECTIVE.

Bruised heart and tearful eye
Seek her dwelling-place, and cry
    When, ah, when?
And the steadfast stars reply:
You shall see her when you die—
    Not till then.

WILL.

I.

Art thou he, said the Child to the Man,

    Art thou he that has narrow'd my ways,

And stinted my life to thy plan,

    And darken'd the mirth of my days?

Art thou he that has placed me at school

    To learn what thy minions shall teach ;

That has cow'd me by rod and by rule,

    And order'd my thoughts and my speech?

Art thou he that would have me believe

    In the God whom thy fathers adored ;

That art wont to be angry and grieve

    When I fail in the fear of the Lord?

Go to! I have none of thy needs;
  Thy tasks I shall never fulfil;
I abjure both thyself and thy creeds:
  I adhere to the fact of my will.

II.

Art thou he, said the Woman to the **Man**,
  That has spoken so frankly of me?
That has dared to attempt what he can
  Towards the setting my sisterhood free?

Thou hast help'd us a little in fight,
  Knowing well that the woman who **can**,
'Tis her duty as well as her right,
  To stand on a level with man.

But what then?   Do I owe thee for this
  More thanks than a spendthrift might pay
Who barters his faith for a kiss,
  Or squanders his substance at play?

Not a whit !   I will give thee for thank
  Just this little piece of advice :
Not to think it so wise to be frank—
  Not to offer thy wares without price.

Who gave thee a mission to speak
  Of things that we all of us knew :
How maids should be modest and meek,
  And wives should be tender and true ?

Who bade thee so rashly reveal
  The history of women obscure :
How they think, how they act, how they feel,
  How they suffer, being trampled and poor ?

Not we !   We can listen, indeed ;
  But we know how to pay thee again :
For honour, to those of our breed,
  Does not mean what it means with you men.

Have a care ! If you come to disgrace

None can say that we did it; and still

You may haply be fool'd to your face

By the might of a womanish will.

III.

Art thou he, said the Man to the Man,

That has visions so vapid and vain,

Of an effort, a purpose, a plan,

Running on through these ages of pain ?

Art thou bound to the leaves of a book ?

Art thou clasp'd in the claws of a creed ?

Dost thou hide in some dreary old nook

From the day which is dawning indeed :

From the day that is brighter than youth,

And fairer than beauty or fame ?

The day when impossible Truth

Shall consent to be only a name ;

E

The day when a better new birth
  Shall revive every soul but thine own ;
When no monarch shall reign upon earth
  Save enlighten'd self-interest alone ?

Dost thou flee such a prospect as this,
  And hate it, and sullenly say
That the gloomy old shadows were bliss
  Compared to so dreadful a day ?

Oh ! fool, we have done with the Past,
  And the Future is formless and vague ;
But the Present, the Present, will last :
  All else is a snare and a plague.

Belief ?   Look at Jonah of old
  (You know that ridiculous tale ?) ;
Well, we've got rid of creeds ; and behold,
  Our Jonahs can swallow the whale !

'Tis an excellent diet; you see
   How favour, and power, and gains,
Come thronging to fellows like me,   •
   Who know what to do with their brains.

Then be ruled; do not stand on the brink,
   Waiting long for the impotent thrill
Of a conscience : you have but to think,
   And to act, and to be—what you *will.*

•

OUT OF HEART.

Out of heart, because the times are moving
    Faster than our settled pace can move:
Out of heart, because the art of loving
    Is not perfect as the power to love.

Out of heart, because the folk of station
    Are not earnest, are of shallow mind;
And, for reverence and imagination,
    Those less lofty are but fools and blind.

Out of heart, because the new days o'er us,
    Brilliant doubtless, but severely cold,
Never, never, shall again restore us
    What they take in beauty from the old.

Out of heart, because we are not learning
    Freedom's noblest lesson and her last—
How to rear the fruits of free discerning
    In the stately gardens of the Past.

Out of heart, because no human guiding
    Fits mankind for triumphs that endure ;
Wisdom self-controll'd and self-abiding,
    Purest aims and methods also pure.

Out of heart, because belief is failing,
    Old creeds dead and new ones fond or foul ;
Little left to cheer the weak and ailing ;
    Little left to stay the manly soul.

Out of heart, because ourselves are erring,
    Always feebler than the good we know ;
Much within us still alive and stirring,
    Which might well have perish'd long ago.

Yes, indeed, for many an ample reason

We who live such lives and must depart,

After living thus so short a season,

Well may falter, well be out of heart.

.

But of one thing Time has not bereft us,

One thing is; and, be it weak or strong,

Hold by that, if nothing else is left us:

That, the living sense of Right and Wrong.

OUR CREED.

·

What, you are forty-five, and yet
   Your heart is living still!
A thing which most of us forget,
   Or do our best to kill—

A thing not worth your while to heed,
   Much less to prate about;
Which even women scarcely need,
   And men are best without.

'Gad, Sir, some error of your life
   Has left this dross with you;
Perhaps you've wed a weakly wife,
   So you've grown weakly too?

Come, look at me; I'm cool in head,
    And clear in brain, you know;
And why?   Because my heart was dead,
    Thank goodness! long ago.

What says your Shakespeare in the play?
    He gives my verdict, too:
For, "Throw the worser part away,
    And then," says he, "you'll do!"

That fellow Shakespeare's right, for once;
    And as his words advise,
All, save the idiot and the dunce,
    Will act, if they are wise.

For what is life?   *Success,* my friend—
    And evermore *Success!*
Ask, Is not that its aim and end?
    And all will answer, Yes!

But who the devil can succeed,
   Whatever be his part,
If in the race of thought and deed
   He's weighted with a heart?

That spoils his work before it's done;
   That cancels half his gains;
He cannot live till that is gone—
   Because he lives by brains.

And what have brains to do with heart?
   Why, to the clever few,
They're just the power and the art
   Of using fools like you!

Brains, fed with knowledge of the time,
   And heedfully employ'd,
Can help a man to climb and climb
   O'er other men destroy'd.

Brains have help'd *me* to wealth and blood,

In spite of all your airs ;

And if you like it, well and good—

And if you don't, who cares ?

EXPEDIENCY.

Maid of the dim mistrustful eye,
The measured smile, the well-timed sigh,
I think I know when thou art nigh—
    Expediency !

When generous natures, frank and bold,
See suffering wrought by steel or gold,
And cry *Avenge !* Thou criest *Hold*—
    Expediency !

When fervent spirits wait and wait
To do some service for the State,
Thy wisdom—leaves them to their fate,
    Expediency !

When buoyant youth, full fond and fain,
Strives upward still, nor strives in vain,
Thy voice recalls him to the plain,
　　　Expediency !

When lofty age proclaims on high
Some newer true philosophy,
Thy careful prudence whispers *Why ?*
　　　Expediency !

When faith, made strong by some pure creed,
Would dare and do, would fight and bleed,
Thou will dissuade her from the deed—
　　　Expediency !

When rapt affection yearns to make
Some sacrifice for Love's sweet sake,
Thou bidst her from that trance awake—
　　　Expediency !

Not seldom is thy counsel sought;

Not few the teachers thou hast taught;

Thou hast not tamed the world for naught—

    Expediency !

Dear as the fruit is to the tree,

Dearer than freedom to the free,

Art thou to some—but not to me,

    Expediency !

REFLECTIVE.

1888.

Full swiftly stride the evil years,
  And they were best away,
If all their dangers and their fears
  Would pass as swift as they.

But, no, the dangers threaten still,
  And still the fears increase:
They mar our lightest hours, and kill
  The memory of our peace.

Once the bright age moved stately by
  With honour, with renown;
And all our land was harmony,
  And Virtue held her own;

And those who toil'd and those who fought,
   Wherever they might roam,
Still glow'd with one undying thought—
   That England was their home.

Ah, how unlike the days we see!
   An England soil'd and worn,
Where Wisdom scarcely dares to be,
   And Hope is left forlorn;

Where no man fears the settled fate
   Of him who loves a lie;
And no man knows, that every State
   Must be at one, or die.

ILLUSIONS.

What, said the wise old World, wilt thou never have
    done with illusions?

Art thou a weakling still, always in tears or at
    play?

Spending thy heart, like a child, on the broken toys
    of remembrance,

Or upon stars that shine mockingly, dimly above?

Inaccessible stars! thou hast no wings to attain
    them:

Inaccessible years! never again to be thine.

Leave them: neither expect, nor greatly care to
    remember;

Only come forth and do whilst it is called to-day:

Work is the life of a man, and facts are the food of
    his spirit :

Facts, that are swarming around ; work, that is here
    to be done.

Thus, thou art strong and alive with the breath of
    the warm live Present ;

Thus, thou art seen all around, clear in a shadowless
    noon ;

But if thou darest abide with fancies misty-colossal,

Or among churchyard lights flickering over a grave,

Then shall the far-away Past, or the fatuous hopes of
    the Future,

Hurry thee out of thyself, hither and thither at will.

Out of myself ? O, World, wise World, prolific of
    counsel,

This, then, is all thy word, this is thy message to me !

If they can bear me away from Self that is slave to
    the Present—

F

Future and perish'd Past, how should I welcome
them both !

Yea, and they do: they arouse a nobler self and a truer

Out of this shallow thing, troubled and tainted by thee;

And from thine arduous dreams, and the press of
thy hurrying phantoms,

They can deliver it well; they, and they only, can save.

What are thy boasted facts, and this work that thou
settest before us—

Science with all her crafts, preaching and talking and
trade ?

They may be good by kind; but the man who is
buried among them,

Can he be lord of his soul ? Can he be fully alive ?

Life, that hath light and shade, and Memory, which
is its shadow,

How can they flourish at all, steep'd in thy shadowless noon ?

Flowers and birds are awake in the cool pure prime
  of the morning;
Perfume and song revive under a mellowing eve;
But in the hot faint glare, in the blinding blaze of
  the mid-day,
Nature and Love lie dead, Passion and Melody cease.
So, when the Future appears, far off in the glow of
  her grandeur,
How is she naked and clear, tender and lovely of
  hue!
All who behold her rejoice, for they hear the music
  of angels
Haunting her down to the earth, hasting her on to
  be born.
Yet, when she is so born, and men can say she is
  Present,
Straight her visage is marr'd, batter'd, and broken,
  and changed;

None do worship her now, and they who had
   yearn'd for her, hate her,
'Till in our sight she dies; dies on the cross of her
   shame.
Is she then dead?   Oh, no; she lies in the grave for
   a season,
Wins from a few sad hearts weeping and mourning
   and woe;
But, ere once they have found a tomb that is worthy
   to house her,
She shall arise again, perfected into the Past:
She shall arise, and ascend to a growing and limit-
   less glory;
Glory that none may eclipse, vivid and stable and sure;
Glory that never shall end; for the Present alone is
   illusion;
That which is real is far, that which is true is unseen.

FALLENTIS SEMITA VITÆ.

There was a man, in days gone by,
Whose heart tormented him mightily,
Because the ways of his time were such
That for all his wishing and wearying much
    He could not feel alive.

They are alive, and only they,
Whom Truth hath found and fetch'd away
From self into simplicity
To work her will and thrive thereby
    As human souls should thrive.

But Truth is peaceful, and Truth is one :
And he saw nothing under the sun
But a hopeless tangle of words and deeds,
An endless battle of schools and creeds —
    A dreary strife and dull.

The friends and the foes, they groan'd or cheer'd ;

And the standers-by, some laugh'd, some sneer'd ;

And the rest went forth and took no heed,

For they did not fight for school or creed,

   But to fill their bellies full.

The Popery folk went proudly by

With their sensuous worship of ear and eye ;

Yet the worshippers' hearts were hearts of fire,

Fill'd with a saintly pure desire

   For the things of a spirit-land.

And the Protestant folk, to them was given

A simple faith that went straight to heaven ;

Yet their worshippers' hearts were foul with ire,

Fill'd with a narrow and fierce desire

   For a sword and a strong right hand.

And they who offer'd their novel array

To make up for the faith that was passing away,

What is this gear their prophet sells ?

'Tis the old, old yoke, and without the bells—

  'Tis the cross, but not the crown.

And they who ground the Godhead small,

And held that knowledge was all-in-all,

That the spirit of man must take its chance

In a world of bettering circumstance

  Of knowing what can be known,

Large was the look of their lofty pride ;

Clear and splendid and open-eyed ;

Yet they only shone remote and far,

Remote as the vaguest nebula-star,

  On his soul that long'd for light.

So the world of speech was ever at strife :

But the mute world lived a wholesome life,

And glow'd or gloom'd at even and morn

As if we men had never been born

  Or never had learnt to fight.

" I will arise and go," said he,

" And ask of this hateful mystery,

Why Nature's purpose is not like ours ;

For she never wastes her matchless powers

  In struggles without an end.

" Her rain comes down on the earth's dry crust,

Her sun shines forth because he must ;

Her stars are bright in a frosty sky,

Her waters roll most bounteously,

  For foeman or for friend ;

" Her thunder even, that clears the air,

And her winds that sweep the forest bare,

And her secular changes, vast and wild,

If yet they are hard to be reconciled,

  We see that they work for good :

" They work their work and have done with it :

And the blue sky suffers never a whit,

And over a dead world, soon or late,

The creatures spring and germinate,

   And the earth renews her blood.

" I said I would seek to Nature's shrine :

But I dare not, since she is thus divine;

How could I ask of a Power like this,

So wise, so mighty, so passionless,

   Why her ways are not like ours ?

" Should I say to her stately forest trees

That gather a blessing from every breeze,

' What is the creed your sap receives ?

Which are your philosophic leaves,

   Or your Christian buds and flowers ? '

" ' Fool ! ' they would answer —and even now

I hear their voice in each rustling bough—

' We are at one with our mother the Earth :

She gives us life, and she gives us birth,

   And she gives us a timely grave.

" ' But you, who talk of we know not what,

Who say you have something that we have not,

Alas, if the thing that makes you men

Be this that sets you at odds again,

　'Tis a thing we would not have!' "

Such was the voice that came to him,

That man with the troubled heart and dim;

And he cried aloud in his misery

" Oh, shallow and sordid our souls must be

　That cannot feel alive!

· " There lives more life in a summer day,

In the flight of a bird that wings its way

Joyously under the greenwood glades

Where Beauty bides in her own sweet shades,

　Than truth can ever give!

" Truth? It is true, as I said in youth,

That Beauty herself is the only truth:

Beauty, who dwells with Nature there

In the clear cold calm of the open air,.

   Alone and undefiled.

" Surely, by her may a man get free

From self into simplicity :

Surely, the soul that cleaves to her

By priest nor yet philosopher

   Shall never be beguiled.

" Yea !   For we know what we cannot prove :

And knowledge itself is less than love:

And he who loves shall feel alive,

For sacred Beauty to him shall give

   The heart of a little child."

A PILGRIMAGE.

I went in search of God
 O'er all the hallow'd ground
That Saints have ever trod ;
 But He would not be found.

I sought Him then in vain
 In every meeting-place
Where men expect to gain
 Some glimpses of His face :

I sought Him yet once more—
 Among the wise of heart;
But if they knew His lore,
 They only knew in part :

And those who knew it best,

   How blank they seem'd and **dim,**

When shameless they confess'd

   They nothing knew of *Him !*

So then I turn'd aside

   Toward that favour'd few

Whose faith is firm and tried,

   Whose lives are tense and true :

For where should He be seen,

   If not with such as these ?

How saintly, how serene,

   They seem'd, when on their knees !

And some were so indeed :

   Yea, all were most sincere ;

But then, they felt no need

   To be as others were ;

And so, no heart could raise
  Their narrow thoughts and low :
They knew His clearer ways—
  Himself they could not know.

Ah, then I sank at length
  To languor, to despair :
I had no heart nor strength
  To seek Him anywhere :

For, did not every road
  My weary soul had trod—
The narrow, like the broad—
  Still lead away from God?

Then something said to me
  " Since thou no more can'st roam,
Surely 'tis time to see
  What cheer thou hast at home :

" 'Tis time to understand,

  Since He will have it so,

That God is close at hand

  Whether thou wilt or no;

" That spite of all thy sin,

  Which lies to Him most bare,

His kingdom is within,

  And He Himself is there."

POEMS ON NATURE AND THE SEASONS.

ECHOES.

Sweet Echo, throned above the lucid wave,
      Within thy resonant cave,
What is this place, sweet Echo, dost thou know ?
      She answer'd, *No.*

Then, if thou know'st not, tell us at the least
      For whom this glorious feast
Of form and colour, this fair scene, is spread?
      She answer'd, *Read.*

How can we read ?　For neither tree nor flower,
      Nor rock, nor ruin'd tower,
Unfolds its hidden legend to our eyes?
      She answer'd, *Rise !*

What, shall we climb thy crag, and there perchance
See plainly at a glance   ·
Some mansion, gay with many a gilded vane?
She answer'd, *Vain!*

Must we then rise in stature of the heart,
Till Earth in every part
Seems fill'd with pathos and with poetry?
She answer'd, *Try.*

So shall we learn, by any sight or sound
Of this green vale around,
Who own its beauty and its power to bless?
She answer'd, *Yes.*

And will each soothing sound and sober sight
Be felt with more delight
By him who owns the land, or by ourselves?
She said, *Yourselves.*

Ah ! then, fair Nature's joys are his alone

    Who wins them for his own

By insight, not by ownership at all ;

    Love her but wisely, and she gives them all—

        Said Echo, *All.*

Κύπρις ἢ Ἵμερος.

What are these shadows from the sky
That move about us as we lie
Here by the brimming sluice that leads
Sweet water through the watermeads ?
   'Tis but the image of some bird—
Another, and again a third—
That sails across the quiet blue
Enjoying life as we may do.
   Cloudless the heaven is near and far,
And lucid as the waters are ;
Sunshine is o'er us and around,
Upon the trees, upon the ground ;   ·
And sunny bubbles dance and quiver
Along the sluice, along the river ;

And rainbow-like the sunlit spray

Rises and floats and drifts away

Above the rolling waterwheel.

Ah, who in such a time could feel

Less bright, less pure, less calm and still

Than yon fair pool beyond the mill,

Where never weed nor flake of foam

Hath leave to make itself a home

Or even seek a resting-place ?

    Yea truly—on the placid face

Of that clear pool a summer sky

Reflects its own benignity :

But in the pool's dark depths (you know)

In gloomy hollows far below

The crumbling edges of the dyke

Dwells that inexorable pike,

The terror of our upland stream ;

Whom roach and barbel, dace and bream,

Abide not, but forsake in fear

A spot to us and them so dear.

We too, in spite of outward ease,

Have our own secret enemies

Who from within can drive away

All timid thoughts that fain would stay

And occupy with milder art

The stillness of a vacant heart ;

We too have shadows of the brain

Flung by some passing joy or pain

That is but near to nothingness,

And yet hath substance form and stress

Enough to cast a varying shade

On whatsoever may be laid

Beneath it as the shadow moves.

'Tis Aphrodite with her doves :

· 'Tis Aphrodite in the air—

'Tis Aphrodite everywhere.

GRACILIS AMNIS.

Do I miss thee, little river,
   Here beside the boundless sea,
Where such mighty waves deliver
   Mightier messages to me?

Where the storm-clouds, huge and hoary,
   And the lightning, and the rain,
And the sunlight in its glory
   March and mingle o'er the main;

Where from such tremendous sources,
   Free, unfathom'd, and unknown,
Nature gathers all her forces
   Just to mock me with my own?

What care they, securely dealing
With this puny world of ours,
What care they for human feeling,
Human life, or human powers?

Yes, I miss thee, little river;
·Thou, at least, hast gifts for me:
And the gifts are like the giver—
Full of fair tranquillity.

What a contrast, little river,
Is thy still and soothing flow,
And the trees that o'er thee quiver,
And the flowers that by thee grow,

What a contrast to the splendour
Of the passion-haunted sea,
Too majestic to surrender
Any love to such as me!

AUTUMN LEAVES.

I.

Who cares to think of autumn leaves in Spring ?
　When the birds sing,
And buds are new, and every tree is seen
As in a mist of tender gradual green ;
　And every bole and bough
Makes ready for the warm low-brooding wings
Of nested ones to bosom there and prove
　How sweet is Love :
Alas, who then will notice or avow
　Such bygone things ?

II.

For hath not Spring the promise of the year ?
　Is she not always dear

To those who can look forward and forget?

    Her woods do nurse the violet;

With cowslips sweet her dewy fields are set;

    And varnish'd butterflies

    Gleam in her gleaming skies;

And life looks larger as each lengthening day

Draws off the shadow and drinks up the tear:

Youth shall be youth for ever; and the gay

High-hearted Summer with her pomps is near.

III.

'Yes, but the soul that meditates and grieves,

    And guards a precious Past,

And feels that neither joy nor loveliness can last;

To her the fervid flutter of our Spring

Is like the warmth of that barbarian hall

To the scared bird, whose wet and wearied wing

Cross'd it just once, and came not back at all.

Poor shrunken soul, she knows her fate too well ;

   Too surely she can tell

That each most delicate toy her fancy made,

And she herself, and what she prized and knew,

   And all her loved ones too,

Shall soon lie low, forgotten and decay'd

   Like autumn leaves.

INGS.

Cold floods have fill'd the vale,
   Both marsh and meadow ground ;
Our firmest footings fail,
   Our summer paths are drown'd.

Beneath a howling sky
   Rude winds alone are heard ;
They hear no lover's sigh,
   Nor song of mated bird.

The leaves we loved in Spring
   Are floating fast to sea,
Or deep in mould they cling ;
   More fruitful thus than we.

The ruddy moon so fair,
   That in the east should rise,
Grey mists have gather'd there
   To hide her from our eyes.

What means this sad deray?
   What means this cloudy pall?
Alas! no skill can say
   The lesson of it all.

But one poor truth is plain
   This dark December day:
That nothing comes again
   Which once hath pass'd away.

APOCALYPSE.

Some years go by so comfortably calm,
  So like their fellows, that they all seem one;
Each answering each, like verses in a psalm,
  We miss them not—until the psalm is done;

Until, above that mild responsive strain,
  An alter'd note, a louder passage rolls,
Whose diapason of delight or pain
  Ends once for all the sameness of our souls;

Until some year, with passionate bold hand,
  Coerces quite our languid liberty,
And changes, in a moment's swift command,
  All that has been, and all that is to be.

Thenceforth, the new year never comes unheard;

    No noise of mirth, no lulling winter's snow,

Can hush the footsteps which are bringing word

    Of things that make us other than we know.

Thenceforth, we differ from our former selves;

    We have an insight new, a sharper sense

Of Being; how unlike those thoughtless elves

    Who fear no fate, and watch no providence!

We watch, we wait, with not a star in view;

    Content, if haply whilst we dwell alone

The memory of something live and true

    Can keep our hearts from freezing into stone.

A FAREWELL TO THE NORTH.

The summer days so warm and still,
  The summer nights so fair;
The dews that gleam'd in Raincliff woods
  When we were rambling there;

The autumn suns, that set in flame
  Beyond that purple wold,
And blazed upon our ruddy roofs,
  And turn'd our becks to gold;

All these are gone, and earth and sky
  Resume their wintry hue:
All these are gone for evermore,
  And we are going too.

THE SEASONS.

Fast bound within the flying train
   I see yon moon arise,
And move to light my native land
   And crown my native skies.

Full fair to-night that moon will shine
   Upon the Northern Sea;
But I who loved her am not near,
   She will not shine for me.

And yet, through all the frosty months,
   And all the winter's snow,
Far down upon the sounding beach
   Our lads will come and go;

And many a lusty lass and brave
   O'er cliff and scar will roam,
To gather for the men at sea
   What things they need from home;

And Mary's cheek will glow the more,
　　And Annie's babe will thrive,
And ancient Alice from her chair
　　Will see the boats arrive;

And long before the gales are done
　　Or bluer skies appear,
I know there will come surely on
　　(Sweet words!) another year.

Another year! My far-off friends,
　　Your hearts are warm and true,
But not so oft you'll think of me
　　As I shall think of you;

And, though to-day is dead and gone,
　　And though we cannot see,
Among the trodden paths around,
　　That path which is to be;

I will not think my feet can fail

    From off their wonted shore ;

I go—for months and years I go,

    But *not* for evermore.

LOVE LYRICS AND POEMS.

MAIDEN ALICE.

Maiden Alice sits alone
   In the woods above the stream
Resting on a mossy stone
   Dreaming there her summer dream

Waters spring beneath her seat
   Leap and trickle down the glen
Ladyfern o'er head and feet
   Keeps her safe from questing men

While the larger brook below
   Rolls a liquid lullaby
And the wavering tree tops show
   Glimpses of a quiet sea

In her dreams came one she knew

(Who it was she could not tell)

Came and stole sweet kisses two

Came and said he loved her well

Then she woke within a while

Startled by the seabird's scream

And she answer'd with a smile

There was nothing in the dream

But the man who loved her best

He who thought her fairest fair

Had pursued his tender quest

Till he found her waking there

And he came with stealthy tread

Soft between the sheltering trees

And above her dainty head

Dropp'd a rose upon her knees

Then she looked aloft and there

Saw her fancied love again

Stooping o'er her loosened hair

Making sure of kisses twain

Lo (he said) the things of sleep

Oft are truer than they seem

You whom I have caught and keep

Was there nothing in your dream ?

AN ENCOUNTER.

Here we meet beside the river,
By the slowly-sliding river,
  Where a boat is seldom seen ;
Only hedgerow birds can hear us,
Only leaping fish are near us,
  And the very path is green.

Is there aught around, above you,
That can look at and not love you ?
  If there be, it is not I ;
All the time you stand before me
You are passing through and o'er me—
  But you shall not pass me by !

Don't you see the path is narrow—

Scarce the width of Cupid's arrow—

And there really is not room?

Therefore, do not wince or waver,

For 'tis kissing's out of favour.

When the gorse is out of bloom!

NAUGHTY NELLY.

So sweet she is, so sweet and fair,
Such glow and glory grace her hair,
I often used to wish she were
   A little more divine.

I sadly wish'd in her to see
A little less of giggling glee,
A little less of coquetry,
   And pertness, and design.

I wish'd that she had learnt at school
Not how to win men and to rule
By making wise ones play the fool,
   And foolish ones adore ;

But how to use the charms she had

In cheering hearts that else were **sad,**

And making one heart always glad

    And blest for evermore.

I wish'd—but wishing is a trade

For boys and simple maidens made;

And if I tried it, I'm afraid

    I could not set her free

From all the tricks and trumperies

That keep her nature in disguise,

And will not let her cast her eyes

    On quiet folks like me.

HARTLIP WOODS.

The roses are out and the lilac is over,
    The cherries are reddening fast on the tree ;
The purple pea-bloom leads us on to the clover—
    And when is my sweetheart a-coming to me ?

I saw her when Winter was whitening round us,
    And Nature's green promise lay hid in the snow,
I look'd far away from the frost world that bound us,
    And said, She must come, I had long'd for her so!

I saw her in Spring, seeming nearer and brighter—
    All flowers, all blossoms, spake of her to me ;
And the orchards above were not purer or whiter
    Than she whom I look'd for in Summer would be.

And now it is time, for the harvest is nearing;
    Yet still she abides in some maidenly home;
I see not a sign of her instant appearing:
    Oh, must I believe she is never to come?

Must I think I have seen but some dainty delusion,
    Unreal as Hope, unsubstantial as Joy,
Still luring me on, to my shame and confusion,
    From useful endeavour, from eager employ?

Ah, then, 'twill be sorrow enough to remember
    That fancies were folly, that passion was vain;
That the roses of June nor the fruits of September
    Can never give me any pleasure again;

That when Autumn has come and all gleaning is ended,
    And the glooms that betoken fresh Winter appear,
I may die, as I live, unbeloved, unbefriended—
    The last lonely leaf of a desolate year.

I

IFS AND BUTS.

If,I had seen her when she was a child,
   And loved her girlhood as I loved her age,
   And help'd to build her up through every stage
Of well-attemper'd structure, undefiled

By the rash hands of raw artificers ;
   If I had known her as I know her now,
   And understood the awe of her white brow,
And that heroic ardour which is hers

By right of youth, whose passion, still unspent,
   Can neither brook the stillness and the grey
   Of lives autumnal, nor that sober way
Wherein they walk toward Death, and are content :

If I had felt how much she needed more

   Than my slow heart could give and rigid mind,

   I should not thus have had to stay behind

And watch an ebbing tide upon a lonely shore.

But man who first loves woman in his prime—

   Whose love comes suddenly on him like a storm

   O'er darken'd noons in summer—can he form

His settled self to suit the foregone time

When she lived on without him? Can he learn

   How fared her youth, and by what steps she grew

   To be a thing so loveable, so new,

Startling with manifold grace at every turn

His strong maturer self? Ah, he may move

   Her heart to yield ; but no interpreter

   From God can ever teach both him and her

To read alike the characters of love.

ALTER ET IDEM.

Here is the ancient stream,
Gliding so smooth and still
Over dark earth and slippery stones
To the mill-race above the mill.

Thirty years ago,
When Mary and I were young,
We used to sit by this very stream,
While the throated throstles sung.

Thirty years ago
We sat, and we made our vow ;
Each to the other and hand in hand,
On the spot where I am now.

But twenty years ago,

    When I came back from far,

And look'd and long'd for the day to come

    That shows what women are,

I found another here;

    A maid, but it was not she :

She had wedded the man that pleased her **most,**

    And she had not wedded me.

Well, 'twas a weary time

    For a girl like her to wait :

Ten years is a long and a weary time

    For a woman to want her mate.

And yet, it only seems —

    Now that I know how it ends —

It only seems such a little while

    Since Mary and I were friends !

Ah, I know how it is

With women as well as with men ;

Their hearts fly back to the days of old

And prick them, now and then.

They are rapt into love once more ;

They are prick'd with a passing pang,

When they think sometimes of a shady stream

Where the throated throstles sang.

But where are the waters now

That flow'd past Mary and me ?

And where is the check on a human soul

Which moves and must be free ?

For love dies down in the heart,

As the flesh rots from the bones :

And under the stream I still can see

All that is left of those days to me ;

Dead earth, and the slimy stones.

PARTED.

Why are your eyelids warm with tears
  While mine are dry and cold?
Why thrill you so with hopes and fears
  At all that you behold,

While my unhappy soul endures
  The good things and the bad,
And is most callous still, though yours
  Be joyous or be sad?

You seem so weak, yet are so strong!
  Your vividness and grace
Embolden right and baffle wrong
  Through all your dwelling-place.

What would I give to enter in
  Where your light footsteps cease;
To feel your energy within,
  And be, like you, at peace !

How can you be so firm and true
  And tranquil as you are,
And not make me as tranquil too,
  And tenderer by far ?

Ah, but I know !   There's nothing strange
  In wonders such as these:
It is not that I cannot change,
  Or you no longer please :

It is not that my heart is cold
  To pity and distress,
Or that I care not as of old
  For truth and righteousness.

No, it is *you!* You would not be

    What once you all but were;

You took your love away from me,

    And left no other there.

So, though to your pure life and laws

    My memory is most true,

You cannot help me now; because

    I have no part in you.

TOO LATE.

I would not woo, nor wed,
   For wasting of my prime:
I scorn'd my heart, and said
   To-morrow was her time;
To-morrow, not to-day,
   Such busy souls as mine
Might fling some hours away,
   Might some high hopes resign,
      For her,
That fretful heart divine,
   That fond idolater.

She yielded to my will :
    Yet not at once she died ;
Oh, long she struggled still,
    Oh, long she yearn'd and sigh'd !
But I, imperious grown
    With honours and with fame,
Had strength to thrust her down
    And hush her bitter blame,
        Till she
Lay heap'd with squalid shame
    Far out of sight in me.

And time serenely roll'd ;
    And all the world was kind ;
And I grew sleek with gold,
    And mellow-ripe in mind ;
Until, by evil chance,
    I saw a vision sweet :
With self-forgetting glance,
    With soft unshadow'd feet

And shy,
I saw the wraith advance
Of young Simplicity.

Then to my heart I cried
That long was bound in me,
" I will no more deride
Thy loves, oh heart, and thee :
Though once I wish'd thee dead
And would not let thee thrive,
Thou art of heavenly seed,
Thou surely art alive :
Then come,
Arise, and let me lead
My youth's fair fancies home."

Yes ; she arose, and broke
Her bondage and was free ;
But ah, she only spoke
These fearful words to me :

" Too late !   Thou art removed

Beyond what I can cure ;

Thou never hast been loved ;

Thou art not meek nor pure.

Oh, fool !

To love, and to endure,

Is better than to rule."

EPITHALAMIUM.

Winter is over and gone: Ah! me, what a desolate
 yearning
All of us lately have felt, wishing that winter were
 past !
Winter is passing indeed, and Spring with its joys is
 returning ;
Sunshine and beauty and life visit our dwelling at last.

Oh! then what bliss there will be, in the beautiful
 haunts of the valley,
Watching the leaves as they come, watching the
 flowers appear ;
Walking in warmth and light, and loving to linger
 and dally,
Ever with eager hearts, sharing the growth of the year.

Full are our placid streams; and the peaceful ponder-
 ing cattle
Stand by the riverside, taking their portion of ease:
Taking it calmly and slow, for they reck not of life
 as a battle;
Nay, for to them 'tis a feast: provender up to the knees.

We, too, gazing abroad on the woods and meadows
 around us,
We have our portion of joy; we, too, can gather it there:
Gazing far further afield, beyond the horizons that
 bound us,
Over the height of the Downs, into the musical air.

Is not our churchyard hill, where it looks on the
 wandering waters,
Is it not haunted by Her, fairest and best of her time?
Do we not know of a truth that *She* still lives in her
 daughters—
Onward from grace to grace guiding them up to their
 prime?

Sorrow has been with us all; but joy, in a wonderful
   fashion,

Grows from the rooted Past, springs to the heart, to
   the tongue:

Joy in another's joy—in the thought of an innocent
   passion

Born at the fount of Love, into the souls of the
   young.

We, who have sorrow'd and lost, we still can
   rejoice with another

Not by our years outworn, not by our follies beguiled:

We, who have known what a charm there was once
   in the life of the mother,

Now shall behold it again, here in the face of her
   child.

SONNETS.

.

K

A DEAD QUEEN.

Here dwelt she, with the husband of her youth :
"A daughter of the gods, divinely tall
And most divinely fair," she gave to all
Her lovely presence, and the tender ruth

Of sympathy and succour; with such truth
And earnestness she gave it, that the gift
Out of ourselves ourselves had power to lift,
And make the roughness of our sorrow smooth.

Ah, still she gives it! Such a gracious thing
Was that fine rapture of ethereal joy
Wherein she moved, that all the shores of Love
Still echo with its music ; and do sing
To us, in tones that nothing can annoy,
Of Her, who is around us and above.

.

RHODODACTYL.

To rise by moonlight of a winter's day
    And see the soft mists lie like folded lawn
    On stream and valley, not to be withdrawn
Till all those black moon-shadows pass away ;

To watch the skies grow clearer, and the grey
    Melt eastward into colour—thinly strawn
    Amber and rose, that through a cloudy dawn
Suffused, shall make it beautiful as they :

In such a twilight glow, to walk abroad
    Beyond the garden and the avenue
Up to yon heath, where by a quiet road
    Our Druid Stone stands central to the view
And sees the sunrise : Ah, what we have owed
To this !   For we have seen the sunrise too.

INCEDIT REGINA.

From her long, languid, dull monotony
   Of leafless days awakes our budding year ;
   It is the old, old story : doubt and fear,
Sun-gleams that vanish in a clouded sky,

Are with her at the first ; but presently
   Her light grows calm, her storm clouds move away,
   And in some sweetest hour of some sweet day
She finds, for them who love and can descry

Her moods, a place wherein the harmony
   Of sight and sound, of splendours new and old,
   Fulfils itself in Autumn's peaceful gold.

Ah, no ! There is a discord : suddenly
   Across the fields of harvest we can hear
   Chill winter whirlwinds, piping loud and near.

SORROW.

Sorrow, my guide, my teacher, and my mate,
  To whose divine companionship I owe
  All that I feel and much of what I know,
Think not thou scorn, O Sorrow, that my fate

Hath brought me nigh to such a potentate,
  Yea, such a king, as thou art. Men may grow
  To love the cross they bear; and even so
Should I love thee, whose pomp of sombre state

Is with me always. I have seen thee send
  And pluck his morsel from the lips of Joy
In mid-fruition: yet art thou a friend
  Even to the bliss thou seemest to destroy.
Thou art more tender far, and far more fair,
Than she who else would haunt me—dumb Despair.

ORE TENUS.

From rock to rock, in early hours of hope,
  We climb'd exulting; and by many a fall
  Still undismay'd, we scaled the mountain wall,
And ranged awhile along that upper slope

Where the last Alpine flowers have leave to ope
  Their daring petals to a summer sky;
  And these we cull'd, but could not pass them by,
Nor gain those rarer heights, to see the scope

Of morning from the summit.   Therefore now
  We turn; and each, as he foregoes his share
Of ultimate achievement, sees below
  The common level of distress and care
To which he must descend.   Ah, but we know
  Our Past will still be with us, even there.

DESCENSUS AVERNI.

Nor this nor that, nor any other thing
   Can rouse us, in the autumn of decay,
   To that high rapture of a former day
Wherein we could not but rejoice and sing.

Summer may ripen the crude buds of Spring;
   But we have seen the summer pass away
   Long since, and seen our callow mates grow grey,
And know what fruit Armida's gardens bring.

Chill Winter is already on the air,
   Charged with white storm and loud destructive
   blast :
Nor could our lessening Future seem as fair,
   Though full of calm, and gracious to the last,
As those bright toys for which we used to care—
   The unfulfill'd ambitions of the Past.

MARCH MEADOWS.

A thick white mist lies heavy on the vale—
  Heavy, and soft, and cold : on either hand,
  Ghosts of themselves, the trees and hedges stand,
Nor black nor green, but vaguely dull and pale;
And in the clotted air, our lambs' weak wail
  Is stifled ; and a silent spectral band
  Of cattle moves across the shadowless land,
Wherein all forms are blurr'd, all voices fail.

Ah ! me, how like is this our stern sad Spring
  To Life's yet sterner autumn !   Such a mist,
    So cold, so formless, from the Lethe-stream
Rises and spreads, and blots out everything
    That we have keenly loved and warmly kiss'd ;
    Till we, too, are but figures in a dream.

FLOS FLORUM.

One only rose our village maiden wore;
    Upon her breast she wore it, in that part
    Where many a throbbing pulse doth heave and start
At the mere thought of Love and his sweet lore.

No polish'd gems hath she, no moulded ore,
    Nor any other masterpiece of art :
    She hath but Nature's masterpiece, her heart;
And that show'd ruddy as the rose she bore.

Because that he, who sought for steadfastness
    Vainly in other maids, had found it bare
    Under the eyelids of this maiden fair,

Under the folds of her most simple dress.
    She let him find it ; for she loved him too
    As he loved her : and all this tale is true.

A.D. 1590.

So do they love, Aemilia and her lord,

   That neither knows the other's faults at all

   Save by confession; which may scarce befal,

Because some kiss anticipates the word.

Nor do their virtues larger scope afford

   Of self-delight, or knowledge mutual;

   Since each believes their own too weak and small

To live unaided by the other's hoard.

Thus they abide in childlike ignorance

If either owe the other aught of ill,

Or if the one have anything of good

Except the other.   Oh, most blessed chance,

More subtle-sweet than art, that hath this skill

To blend two souls in such beatitude !

AMORIS INTEGRATIO.

If I might choose, my fellow-servant said,
   And shyly turn'd her glowing cheek away,
   If I might choose, which never till to-day
Was woo'd by man nor by myself betray'd,

I would not be thus shamefast, thus affray'd :
   For neither joy, till now, nor tyrannous love,
   Nor loneliness, did ever me so move
But that I wish'd to live and die a maid.

And yet, she said, I am not so dismay'd
   By that great mystery of married souls,
   Whereby each serves and also each controls,

And either is the other's light and shade,
   As that I could not bring myself to see
   The dear delight of being a part of thee.

VARIUM ET MUTABILE.

She whom I loved, who loves me now no more,
  Hath two conflicting natures in her soul :
  And one of these she gave me ; gave it whole,
And with an innocent emphasis did pour

That self of hers, full-brimm'd and running o'er,
  Into the heart I offer'd her : a bowl
  Homely perhaps, yet neither slight nor foul,
And apt to hold the treasure that it bore.

But then, her other self arose and cried
  Against my gift, against her plenitude
  Of sweet acceptance ; and in alter'd mood

Sudden she flung that lifted bowl aside.
  So, all the love therein, both hers and mine,
  Lies on the sand, blood-red, like wasted wine.

BEATRICE.

(Firenze, 9 June, 1890.)

Some say, fair Beatrice was a name
　　And nothing more, to Dante: 'twas his mind
　　And not his heart that chose her, and design'd
For her pure spirit such an heaven of fame

That none are counted meet to share the same,
　　Save Mary Mother, of all womankind.
　　Wisdom alone—supreme, elect, refined
Into abstraction, was our poet's Dame.

Oh fools ! The master-passion of a soul
So prompt with noble purpose, so absorb'd
In quest of all beneath us and above,

Was it then *nothing* ?　Ah, how false, how foul,
Were such a life, did it not stand full-orb'd
In the warm radiance of a woman's love !

CHRISTMAS.

Our Christmas is a time of make-believe :

  We carol still, we who are growing old,

  Beside the grave wherein lies stark and cold

All that once warm'd and gladden'd Christmas Eve.

Ah, yes ! We do it that we may not grieve

  Our children; lest they also should behold,

  Through mirth and music, amid gifts and gold,

The one sad face that never can deceive—

The face of Sorrow. For on Christmas Day

  Sorrow was born ; who came on earth to die

Vainly: *how* vainly, none, alas ! can say

  Who hath not heard believers strive and cry ;

Who hath not felt, on this bright bitter morn,

That if our God can fail, we too were best unborn.

THE END.